Hast

and
The 1066 Country

featuring
BATTLE, BEXHILL, PEVENSEY, RYE, ST. LEONARDS AND WINCHELSEA

Text: David Arscott   Photography: David Brook

S.B. Publications

ACKNOWLEDGEMENTS

We wish to thank Ann Scott and Dennis Collins for their invaluable help in the conception and development of this book, while happily acknowledging that its failings are all our own.

Special thanks also to:

Hastings Borough Council for their permission to reproduce the Borough Arms and the Common Seal

Victoria Williams, Curator of Hastings Museum

David Hartley of Smugglers' Adventure

Quentin Lloyd for his permission to use the photograph of Great Dixter.

Front Cover: East Hill cliffs and fishing quarter, Hastings.

Title Page: Senlac Hill and Battle Abbey.

Back Cover: Borough Arms of Hastings. The two flags depicted above represent as nearly as possible the standards carried at the Battle of Hastings, and are to be seen flying in Hastings to remind visitors and townsfolk of the events of October 14th, 1066.

Both are depicted in the Bayeux Tapestry — that of William, Duke of Normandy (the Conqueror) being a gold cross on a silver ground. It is thought to have been the Papal Gonfalon presented to him by Pope Alexander II. The same device occurs later in the arms of Jerusalem, at the dawn of the heraldic period. The laws of heraldry today would not allow this combination, but in William's day heraldry had not evolved.

A descendant of the family of William's Standard Bearer lives in Hastings today, as do representatives of other families who came with William — and some who were here before he came.

The golden dragon is based on the famous Dragon Standard of Wessex, and was one of two carried by the Saxons. King Harold's other standard was known as 'The Fighting Man' but this, unfortunately, is not portrayed in the Bayeux Tapestry. The Dragon of Wessex would originally have been hollow and three-dimensional, made probably of leather and silk, encrusted with gold: an awesome sight above King Harold's army.

CONTENTS

INTRODUCTION

'Popular with visitors since 1066' runs the witty Hastings promotional slogan, focusing (sensibly enough) on perhaps the most famous event in English history. The fact is, however, that the area was luring newcomers long before William the Conqueror and his heavily-armed tourists arrived here. Flints and pottery fragments discovered in the 600 acres of Hastings Country Park testify to continuous habitation of this part of Sussex from the palaeolithic period, some 350,000 years ago.

The Iron Age promontory fort on the East Hill dates from about 40BC.

What was the attraction? Early men and women travelled along the ridge tops, away from the dense forests of the Weald clays with their dangerous menageries of bears, wild boar and wolves, and there is high ground in abundance here: the honeycombed cliffs of Hastings are part of the great sandstone belt of the High Weald which sweeps north-west across the county to form the heathy prominence of Ashdown Forest. Those prehistoric visitors would have looked down from the Country Park and from Castle Hill (where a mesolithic settlement has been discovered) to the spreading swamps of what was to become the English Channel, at last separating Britain from the Continent around 6000BC.

Later generations exploited a valuable ore discovered within the stone: iron. The Iron Age chieftains built great fortresses all along the south coast, and the remains of two of them can be seen on the East and West Hills at Hastings. This region was occupied by the Belgae, a people who had themselves been 'visitors' a few hundred years previously and who retained close links with tribes across the Channel.

The Romans, invading in 43AD, prized the area for its iron deposits. A major ironworking site has been excavated in Beauport Park, to the north of Hastings, where the walls of the bath house still stand to a height of seven feet in places. There were other significant works at Sedlescombe, Brede and Crowhurst, and Ordnance Survey maps indicate a great many smaller 'bloomery' sites where charcoal was used to melt the ore into a workable state.

At Pevensey (to them 'Anderida') the Romans built a great fort (*p. 73*) to defend their 'Saxon Shore'. The small enclosure known as 'St. George's Churchyard' on the East Hill at Hastings may be the remains of a signalling station of the same period. These were necessary measures, for the area was yet again proving extremely popular with visiting hordes — in this case, Saxon pirates.

We have only the scantiest knowledge of what happened after the Roman legions withdrew in the early 5th century, leaving coast and countryside at the mercy of land-hungry invaders. A headline, as it were, in the *Anglo-Saxon Chronicle,* tells us that the Saxon chieftain Aelle sacked the fort at Pevensey in 491AD 'and slew all the inhabitants; there was not even one Briton left there'. Aelle is credited with creating the kingdom of the South Saxons, or Sussex, but his writ seems not to have run throughout what we now know as 1066 country. The eastern part of this region was settled by the 'Haestingas', who probably had the natural barriers of the sea, the Pevensey and Romney marshes and the great forest of Andresweald to thank for their independence. Whatever the reasons, we find a much later entry in the *Chronicle* reporting that in 771 King Offa of Mercia subdued both Sussex 'and the men of Hastings'.

The importance of Hastings in Saxon England is evident from the fact that, like Chichester and Lewes, it was the site of a mint with several moneyers, one of them called Dunninc. Remarkably, his descendants still live in the town, the family name being little changed, to Dunk. Coins were produced here in the reigns of Aethelstan, Canute, Edward the Confessor and Harold. The town had a flourishing fishing fleet, and the confederacy of the Cinque Ports (Hastings with the Kent ports of Romney, Hythe, Dover and Sandwich) may have been formed as early as the Confessor's reign.

Certainly Hastings was no isolated backwater at the time of the Conquest. Many of its great estates were owned by Norman lords, religious and secular, and their loyalty to William no doubt influenced his decision to come ashore on this stretch of the English coast. The battle (*p. 76*) might easily have been lost, but Sussex was quickly subdued once it was over. The county was divided into five (later six) administrative areas known as 'rapes', each under the control of a mighty baron and having a stone castle protecting a harbour. Robert, Count of Eu, was responsible for Hastings Castle (*pp. 12-13*), while Robert, Count of Mortain, built another inside the walls of the earlier Roman fortress at Pevensey (*p. 73*).

The early years of Norman rule were a period of prosperity for the area. The Cinque Ports were granted special privileges for providing what was, in effect, the English navy; Hastings and

Saxon coin of Edward the Confessor minted by Dunninc. Actual size 16mm.

The Bayeux Tapestry scene showing King Harold's death: contrary to myth, he is probably not the figure with the arrow in his eye. The knight with the dark shield is carrying the Dragon standard of Wessex. A similar design — a monster with wings, three toes, twisted tail and long ears — also appears on the reverse of the Hastings seal (p.27).

Dover were to supply 21 ships each for fifteen days each year, with the three smaller Kent ports mustering five each. Rye and Winchelsea later joined the confederacy as 'ancient towns', reflecting their own growing importance. Yet, well before the end of the 14th century, these dynamic ports were to shrivel and very nearly die.

There were two principle reasons for this sorry decline, the first being rising sea levels. Large parts of Hastings were washed away, including its harbour, while Winchelsea (*p.80*) was completely inundated and had to be rebuilt on higher ground. (The fickle sea later withdrew, which explains why Pevensey Castle (*p.72*) and the hilltop town of Rye (*p.84*) now stand so far from the water's edge).

Attacks by French pirates during the Hundred Years War (1337-1453) were another scourge of the local population. With the Cinque Ports fleet too weak to protect the coastline, the French murdered almost at will and put the port towns to the torch on several occasions. The stout defensive structures of Bodiam Castle (*p.91*) and the Land Gate at Rye (*p.85*) both date from these troubled times, as do the remnants of the Hastings town wall (*p. 51*).

Hastings, however, continued to earn its living from the sea. The Wealden iron industry, springing to new life with the development of the blast furnace, gave the port trade a boost in the 17th and early

This bottle, now on display at the Shipwreck Heritage Centre in Hastings, still contained red wine when it was brought up from the wreck of the Amsterdam.

18th centuries, and the many displays in the Shipwreck Heritage Centre (*p.45*) testify to the considerable volume of shipping along this stretch of coastline. In times of poverty, moreover, many a local fishing family was tempted to take advantage of high import duties and earn a useful wage from a common but illegal trade — smuggling. The Mermaid Inn at Rye (*p.88*) was a haunt of the notorious Hawkhurst Gang. The Coastguard cottages at Rye and the nearby Coast Blockade watch house, a lookout window in its side tower, are reminders of increasingly successful attempts by the authorities to deal with this rampant lawlessness.

At the very beginning of the 19th century the threat of invasion by Napoleon's forces led to the erection of a chain of so-called martello towers around the south-east corner of England. Several of these remain, including one at Rye and another at Rye Harbour. More ambitious still, however, was the Royal Military Canal, which ran all the way from Cliff End at Pett Level (a few miles east of Hastings) to Shorncliffe in Kent. This was intended as a defensive moat, and its course can still be followed.

The beginnings of the modern era can be traced, symbolically at least, to the building of the celebrated Pelham Crescent under Hastings Castle in 1824 (*p.59*) and to James Burton's creation of a new town by the sea on the western outskirts of Hastings during the same period. St. Leonards (*p.64*) was begun in 1828, and within twenty years the railway had been extended from Brighton, connecting the twin towns with London. Other lines soon followed, bringing the pleasures of promenading and healthy bathing to thousands who had never come within miles of the sea. The phenomenon of the seaside resort had arrived to stay.

Today, although there are pockets of light industry scattered about the Hastings area, although the fishermen still land their catches daily on the Stade, tourism undeniably calls the tune. This can, at its worst, lead to a rash of

Sussex/Kent boundary stone, dated 1806, alongside the Royal Military Canal near Iden. The waterway in the background is the Kent Ditch.

inappropriate entertainments crudely tacked on to the obvious pleasures of coast and countryside: there is, mercifully, little of that here. At its best it encourages the blending of contemporary needs with the preservation of what is most interesting and attractive from the past: a fate which has happily befallen the 1066 country, with its castles and churches, its ancient townscapes and venerable villages.

Hastings itself, for all that it was the most grievously bombed of our Sussex towns during the second world war, retains clusters of beautiful medieval buildings and a Georgian legacy to be proud of. True, the historic Old Town is easily missed by those who rush through with scarcely a glance to right or left. That, however, is a loss they deserve, for this is a feast to be savoured.

The 'black arches' on the East Hill, which seem from a distance to be the entrances to caves, are actually shallow carvings in the rock. The folly is thought to date from the end of the 18th century, when Hastings first began to attract fashionable visitors.

Hastings Old Town from the East Cliff.

HASTINGS and THE 1066 COUNTRY

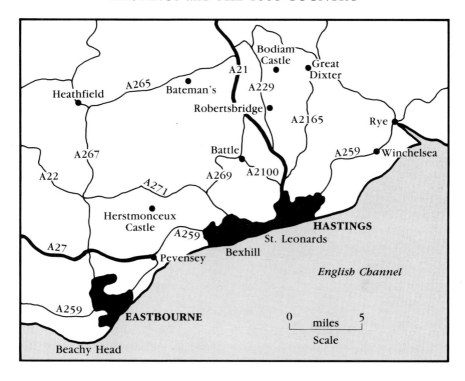

MUSEUMS OF 1066 COUNTRY

Hastings Museum of Local History, High Street 0424 721209
Hastings Museum & Art Gallery, Cambridge Road 0424 721209
Bexhill Museum, Egerton Road 0424 2117691
Court House Museum, High Street, Pevensey
Battle Museum, High Street 04246 3899
Court Hall Museum, Winchelsea
Rye Museum, Ypres Tower, Gun Garden 0797 223254

HASTINGS

Hastings Castle

The Normans built several wooden castles immediately after the Conquest of 1066, and the Bayeux Tapestry shows one at Hastings, but the most strategic of them were later replaced with mighty stone fortresses on high ground which could be easily defended. Hastings Castle, the first of them, was a promontory or cliff-top castle, and the most impressive relic of the construction today lies to the east of the remaining stone walls — the huge ditch which, carved through the sandstone rock, makes this an island site.

Now only a ruin with magnificent views, the castle was once a substantial structure covering eleven acres. We have to imagine it spreading much further to the south over a cliff since eroded by the weather and deliberately cut back to make room for the expanding town below. We must imagine, too, the sea lapping the base of this cliff, for the sea-level was then considerably higher.

The first, timber castle here was probably of the motte-and-bailey type, with a strong keep on an artificial mound looking down on an enclosed courtyard. It was the Conqueror's uncle Robert, Count of Eu, who is thought to have replaced the early defences with stone. There was a collegiate church here which, according to the canons at least, had been founded before the conquest: the fact that the church and its school continued long after the fortifications served any purpose for national defence no doubt accounts for the fact that these are the best-preserved walls today.

Beneath the mound are two arched passageways ending in small chambers. Colourful stories are told about them, but their purpose was almost certainly for storage.

The most substantial remains of Hastings Castle are the walls of the collegiate church. The martyred Archbishop of Canterbury Thomas Becket held the post of dean here for a time.

CASTLES OF 1066 COUNTRY

Hastings (TV 822094); Norman; audio-visual display; open mid-February to end-December

Pevensey (TQ 644048); Roman and Norman; English Heritage: (0323) 762604

Bodiam (TQ 785256); moated, 14th century; National Trust; (085083) 436

Herstmonceux (TQ 646104); moated, 15th century; not open to the public at present

Camber (TQ 922185); Henry VIII castle; under preservation by English Heritage; not open at present

HASTINGS

Smuggling Days

Idle hands among the depressed Hastings fishing fleet found lucrative, if dangerous, work to do during the years of high excise duties in the 18th century when locally-built cutters and luggers were deployed with great skill to outwit the customs men. There is, unhappily, no firm evidence that the caves on the West Hill were used to store contraband, but there's no doubt that the whole area made a healthy living from illicit landings on deserted midnight beaches.

The Hawkhurst Gang, which used the Mermaid Inn at Rye, was the most notorious of a number of well-organised smuggling bands based in the Weald on routes from the coast to the London market. It has been estimated that as much as a quarter of England's overseas trade was being smuggled at this time, and the 1066 country was among the busiest areas of all.

Norman's Bay, Pevensey Bay, Bulverhythe (west of St. Leonards) and Camber were favourite haunts of the 'free traders', men who often behaved savagely towards inadequately armed preventive men and who occasionally paid the price: the Hastings fisherman Joseph Swaine, buried in All Saints churchyard, was shot dead in 1821, while a poor fiddler named Monk was the last smuggler to be killed during a landing, shot by the coastguard at Camber Castle in 1838.

Navigation light on the West Hill, near the entrance to St. Clement's Caves.

Our best contemporary evidence for the extent of smuggling is to be found in the letters written in Hastings by John Collier, a dominant figure in the gradual renaissance of a community which had by this time shrunk to little more than a humble fishing port. Collier, who lived at Old Hastings House in High Street, was not only the town clerk and mayor on several occasions, but the surveyor-general of riding officers.

The establishment of the Coast Blockade and, later, the Coast Guard service helped to suppress organised smuggling, which was effectively brought to an end with the introduction of free trade policies after 1840.

Of the many buildings in Hastings which claim smuggling associations, note West Hill House near St. Clement's Church. This was the home of the most flamboyant of the smugglers and privateers, William Wenham.

St. Clement's Caves have been a paying attraction since 1827, when Joseph Golding dug out new galleries and organised colourful events in the so-called 'ballroom'. He also sculpted a large figure (right), which is popularly believed to represent Napoleon. The caves currently house a smuggling exhibition.

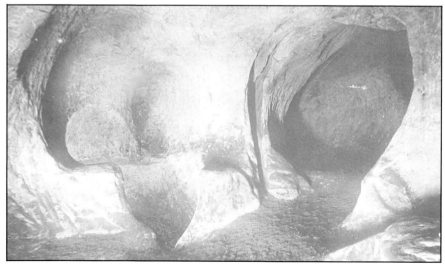

The Roman Bath, St. Clement's Caves.

HASTINGS

George Street

In medieval times Hastings was contained almost exclusively in the Bourne valley between the East and West hills, and when the town began to spread during the 17th century it could only do so by creeping along the shingle under the cliff west of High Street. George Street was then known as 'the Suburbs', being officially granted its present name (after a former pub) in 1811, and the turning from High Street was called Poor Man's Corner.

The houses in George Street have seen many changes of use. A workhouse, for instance, had been established in 1753 on the site of what is now no. 42: the present building was originally the headquarters of the Hastings Literary Institution. Businesses seem to have come and gone with great regularity during the 19th century, among them a number of public houses. There was a school at no. 45, an assembly room at no. 49, the short-lived *Cinque Ports' Chronicle and East Sussex Observer* (1838-40) at no. 55 and the more successful *Hastings and St. Leonards News* (1848-1901) at no. 42.

Perhaps the most distinguished resident was the topographical artist Samuel Prout (1783-1852). He lived at no. 53, which is hidden along a narrow passageway under the West Hill. He suffered penury in his lifetime, having to stay indoors in daylight hours to avoid arrest for his debts, but he is at least honoured with a blue plaque today.

For all that George Street may not be a part of the Old Town proper, it has always been included in the tourist's map of Hastings. A passage next to no. 42 leads to the Hundred Steps that climb to the West Hill and the castle, while the Victorians devised the West Hill cliff railway to take the strain instead.

The 1-in-3 gradient West Hill cliff railway, cut through a natural cave in the rock, connects George Street with Castle Hill. It was built in 1890 and the track is 500ft long.

George Street, now attractively pedestrianised, links the Old Town of Hastings with the modern centre.

HASTINGS

Hastings Twittens

The Old Town of Hastings is cramped between its two massive hills, a fact which contributes substantially to its character. Early builders were forced to colonise every available square foot, even if this meant a steep climb from one of the two main thoroughfares, and glimpses of tucked-away courtyards and gardens perched on rock outcrops are one of the greatest pleasures of walking these streets.

Narrow passageways between houses are known as 'twittens' in Sussex, and the area around St. Clement's Church, between High Street and the West Hill, is rich in such surprises. The roads themselves share this sequestered feeling, running close under the hill or coming to an abrupt halt against its lower slopes.

Exmouth Place was developed at the end of the 18th century, when holidaymakers were first discovering Hastings. There's a plaque on the wall of Rock House to 'one who never turned her back, but marched breast forward': Dr Elizabeth Blackwell, the first woman

Coburg Place, looking towards the caves on the West Hill.

woman to graduate in medicine anywhere in the world. By a strange coincidence, another pioneering woman doctor, Sophia Jex Blake, is remembered by a plaque in Croft Road.

The Croft has a straightness which was originally entirely functional. This was a ropewalk until early in the 19th century, and it's easy to imagine the spinners walking backwards along this unmade road, paying out the hemp that was slung about their waists. The land in this area was to become more profitable for building development, however, and there are some fine houses to be seen along Croft Road and in Gloucester Place, the latter dating from 1817.

Twitten off High Street.

A view along Church Passage.

HASTINGS

St. Clement's Church

It may be the town's oldest church, but St. Clement's has been both moved and rebuilt in its time. It was originally nearer the sea, where it was regularly swamped. Alan the Cheesemonger and his wife Alice provided the present site on higher ground in 1286, but within a century French raiders had reduced the new building to a ruin. Most of the present church therefore dates from about 1380.

The odd shape of the building (the tower at the end of the south aisle, and the nave and north aisle seeming to have been sliced off at the west end) simply reflects the dimensions of the site which the benevolent cheesemonger donated to the town.

John Collier's memorial: 'he acquired an ample fortune with a fair character'. Collier's daughter Mary married Edward Milward, whose family was also to have a profound influence on the development of Hastings.

High on the tower, to either side of the louvre of the bell ringing chamber, are what appear to be two cannon balls. Tradition says that this is, indeed, what one of them was — fired at the church from a Dutch ship during the wars of the 17th century. Its 'mate' was later carved in the stonework for symmetry's sake.

Among the memorials inside the church is one to the John Collier who, apart from five stints as mayor, served as the town clerk from 1706 until 1749. He was one of the canopy-bearers provided by the Cinque Ports for the coronation of George II — a great honour, since the canopy covers the monarch at the supreme moment of anointing. A year after his death, in 1760, the Cinque Ports provided the same privileged service to George III, a fact commemorated by one of two large chandeliers hanging in the nave.

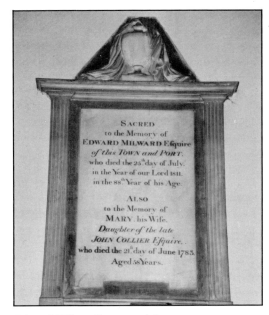

Edward Milward's memorial.

St. Clement's is the borough church of Hastings: there is mayoral pew at the front of the nave, with rests for the two Corporation maces.

St. Clement's Church, off High Street. Its memorials include a framed picture, a sonnet and a sanctuary lamp to the pre-Raphaelite poet and artist Dante Gabriel Rossetti, who married his model, Lizzie Siddal, here in 1860.

HASTINGS

High Street

Until as recently as the 1830s a stream known as the Bourne splashed its way to the sea between the East and West hills, providing the boundary between the ancient parishes of St. Clement's and All Saints for most of its way. The gardens of houses in High Street and All Saints Street ran down to this stream, which had long been the major source of water for Old Town residents, with a water bailiff appointed to keep it clean. Today it flows beneath the ground, giving its name to the road which covers it, and motorists speeding towards Rye are all too likely to miss the now-hidden glories of the town's historic heart.

Not only is High Street lined with old and attractive buildings (there are, for instance, medieval hall houses at nos. 97 and 102-3), but even its raised pavement is architecturally listed! It was known as Market Street until 1814, and the original 15th century Market House can be seen at no. 42a.

Nelson's Buildings in High Street display the great admiral's bust in a niche in the wall. The building was originally a hospital for naval officers during the Napoleonic wars.

What is now the local history museum was the first town hall, built in 1823, with an open market place for its ground floor. Its replacement in 1887 by the present town hall in Queens Road was emblematic of the shift of civic importance from the Old Town to the rapidly developing new centre further to the west.

At the top of the street is the Stables Theatre — built around 1740 as the stables for Old Hastings House nearby.

The old town hall now serves as a local history museum.

The town's first bank opened here in 1791. The tile-hanging on the front conceals some well-preserved 16th century windows.

The Duke of Wellington had his headquarters in this building while commanding a brigade in Hastings during 1806. Another notable soldier, Sir John Moore (see p.56), lodged at 57 High Street while he, too, was stationed in the town.

High Street.

A typical timber-framed house at no. 102 High Street. The gateways in these jettied buildings often lead to picturesque twittens beyond. The raised pavement is itself a listed feature of the Old Town.

The vertical timber struts at first floor level in Dickens Cottage are the (plastered up) remnants of a medieval window: they would have been covered by a curtain or shutters. The cottage is named for the novelist's son, who was a frequent visitor.

THE HASTINGS SEAL

The seal on the facing page is the COMMON SEAL OF THE BARONS OF HASTINGS, as reads the Latin inscription on the obverse. The Freemen of Hastings and other Cinque Ports were known as 'Barons', and jealously guarded their privileges. The seal was probably made during the early part of the reign of Henry III (1216-1272), and can still be used. It is a fine example of the craftsmanship of the period.

It shows a (presumably Hastings) ship cutting an enemy vessel in half. One of the latter's crew can be seen in the water. It may commemorate a famous victory of the time, whose details are lost to us, but it is equally possible that it sounds a warning to any ship seeking to oppose the Cinque Ports! The ship bears both the banner of the Cinque Ports and the royal arms of England, as used before 1339.

The reverse shows St. Michael, the Patron Saint of Hastings, slaying a Dragon.

The inscription has been rendered as "The power of Michael shall overcome thee, oh cruel dragon". The Normans are said to have first entered Hastings on the feast of St. Michael, and a nineteenth century historian has pointed out that St. Michael was known as the 'conqueror of Dragons'. The great fighting standard of the English was The Dragon Standard: that shown in the Bayeux Tapestry is of exactly the type on the Seal (*see back cover*).

HASTINGS

Artists' Hastings

Writers and artists of all kinds have made the 1066 Country their home, and Rye must be counted a leader in the authorial stakes with such as Henry James, Conrad Aiken, E.F. Benson, Rumer Godden and Radclyffe Hall working in the town. Nowhere can compare with Hastings, however, for the range of talents it has attracted to its artistic community.

Putting them in any kind of order would be invidious, though the Victorian poet Coventry Patmore (who lived at Old Hastings House for 15 years from 1876) earns bonus points, as it were, for leaving a bricks-and-mortar legacy in the Roman Catholic church St. Mary Star-of-the-Sea (*opposite page*).

The great English romantic artist J.M.W. Turner, patronised by several of the wealthy Sussex landowners, painted some remarkable scenes of ships off the Hastings coast. Turner was merely a visitor, but the pre-Raphaelite artist and poet Dante Gabriel Rossetti not only lived here but married his model, Lizzie Siddall, in St. Clement's church (where, during the second world war, the best-selling novelist Catherine Cookson was to marry a Hastings Grammar School master). There's a framed picture, a sonnet and a sanctuary lamp to Rossetti's memory inside the church, while Lizzie — who died from an overdose of laudanum two years after the wedding — is buried in the graveyard nearby. Another pre-Raphaelite, Holman Hunt, also stayed in the town.

Locally-based authors have generally had other subjects than the town itself, but the Irish house-painter Robert Noonan, writing as Robert Tressell, left an enduring portrait of working-class Hastings (thinly disguised as Mugsborough) in his novel *The Ragged Trousered Philanthropists,* first published in 1914 and something of a sacred text for the Labour movement. He lived in Milward Road.

A plaque in St. Mary's Terrace shows that it was the home of Archibald Belaney, a Hastings Grammar School boy who, remarkably, turned himself into the Red Indian 'Grey Owl' and wrote a number of colourful books on the wildlife of Canada and its conservation. The mother of the American artist James Whistler lived in the same terrace, and he often visited her there. Old Humphrey Avenue takes its name from the pen-name of George Mogridge, buried close by in All Saints Church. Among the less savoury incomers was Aleister Crowley, dubbed 'the wickedest man in the world' for his diabolism and philosphy of 'do what thou wilt'. He died here in 1947.

The poet Coventry Patmore was a prime mover in the building of the Roman Catholic church St. Mary Star of the Sea, completed in 1882. The architect was Basil Champneys. The interior is impressively large, with vaulting, a high clerestory and a balcony.

HASTINGS

Old Hastings House and the Rebirth of Hastings

Although it was probably built shortly before he arrived in the town (and may have been superimposed upon a timber-framed Tudor building), Old Hastings House is most strongly associated with John Collier, the man whose careful management was responsible for transforming Hastings from a decaying backwater into a prosperous seaside resort. It was known as The Mansion in those days. Collier, a solicitor whose father ran the Lamb in Eastbourne's Old Town, lived here from 1706 when he was appointed town clerk. For all of thirty-nine years he was to be the dominant figure in the civic and business life of Hastings, holding a range of public offices and enriching himself (though with no hint of improper behaviour) through shrewd property deals and money-lending. His letters are a vital source of information about the growth of the newly-confident town he helped to create.

Collier terraced the gardens of Old Hastings House and established a rabbit warren in the sandy banks of what is now The Croft. Because the existing stables were too small for his growing needs, he had four small houses demolished to make room for a new, brick building — now The Stables Theatre. Although it was the chief source of drinking water in the town, the Bourne was a polluted stream, periodically flushed by the release of head-water from a dam known as the Slough; after an outbreak of plague in 1735 a local doctor promoted a (controversial) scheme to supply some houses with a clean water supply through elm pipes, and Old Hastings House, unsurprisingly, was one of those which benefited.

The house remained in the related Collier and Milward families until 1876, when the poet Coventry Patmore rented it. It served as a military hospital during the first world war, but lay empty during the second, when it was damaged by German bombs which fell on 'The Wilderness' nearby. It has been an old people's home since 1947.

Old Hastings House, built in its present symmetrical Queen Anne style around 1700, is not quite as large as it appears. The top storey is in reality part of the roof space, the central window on the first floor and alternate lights on the top floor being false. The handsome summer house is a Victorian addition.

Smuggling (pp 14-15) attracted all kinds of people during the 18th and early 19th centuries. Philip Kent, buried in All Saints churchyard (see following pages) was a 'free trader' who became a Hastings schoolmaster.

HASTINGS

All Saints Church

Like St. Clement's Church, All Saints once probably stood much closer to the sea. Certainly the present building dates from the early 15th century, when its outstanding internal feature was created: the Doom painting over the chancel arch. The rest of the original medieval wall paintings were destroyed during a typical Victorian restoration, but here we see Christ sitting on two rainbows between St. John and the Virgin Mary.

Inside the tower, round the central opening designed for lowering the bells, is a highly unusual roundel decorated with the painted carvings of fruit and animals: its exact medieval meaning is unknown. Nearby is a restored board of 1756, with three verses of doggerel outlining fines to be levied on bellringers who broke the rules. From a slightly later period, and propped against the tower wall, is the old parish pump which stood at the junction of Bourne Walk and Waterloo Passage until 1850.

The gravestones outside have had their lettering badly worn by the elements. One is to the fisherman and suspected smuggler Joseph Swaine, shot by a coast blockade officer who was sentenced to death for the killing, though subsequently pardoned. Still remarkably clear, however, is the inscription on a stone by the church door which tells the horrible tale of nine-year-old John Archdeacon's death in 1820:

> *In childish play he teased a mule*
> *Which rag'd its owner's angry soul*
> *And thro' whose cruel blows and spleen*
> *This child so soon a corpse was seen.*

The infamous fabricator of the 1678 'Popish plot', Titus Oates, was a curate here under his father, then the rector of All Saints. He fled the town to escape arrest for perjury.

All Saints Church, on a high point east of the Bourne. As many as seven Hastings churches are mentioned in a document of 1291, several of them since swallowed by the sea. All Saints and St. Clement's (the only two of the seven dedications to survive) were both subsequently moved further inland.

Joseph Swaine's gravestone.

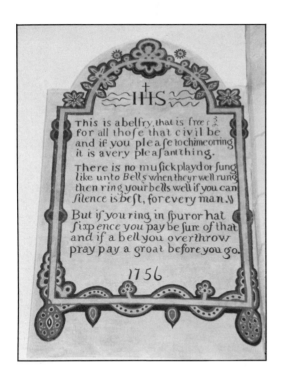

This is a belfry, that is free ʒ
for all thofe that civil be
and if you pleafe to chime or ring
it is a very pleafant thing.

There is no mufick playd or fung
like unto Bells when theyr well rung
then ring your bells well if you can
filence is beft, for every man.ſſ

But if you ring in fpur or hat
fixpence you pay be fure of that
and if a bell you overthrow
pray pay a groat before you go.

1756

The unusual belfry rhymes in All Saints Church reveal that 18th century ringers faced fines both for too much enthusiasm (to 'overthrow' a bell was to snap its wooden stop) and for sloth (arriving so late that they rang 'in spur or hat').

This is a belfry, that is free
for all those that civil be
and if you please to chime or ring
it is a very pleasant thing.

There is no musick playd or sung
like unto Bells when theyr well rung
then ring your bells well if you can
silence is best, for every man.

But if you ring in spur or hat
sixpence you pay be sure of that
and if a bell you overthrow
pray pay a groat before you go.

The old parish pump is propped against the tower wall in All Saints Church. A handle was cranked to draw water from the Bourne Stream.

The medieval painting of the Doom, or Last Judgement, is regarded as one of the finest to survive in England. Note, to one side, a doomed man on the gallows with the Devil hauling on the rope.

HASTINGS

All Saints Street

The medieval twin of High Street, All Saints Street was equally cramped between its hill and the Bourne Stream but somewhat poorer. Today it's every bit as glorious, with its procession of beautifully preserved old buildings, some standing behind (again like High Street) a listed raised pavement.

Just below the church is the 16th century Stag Inn, a tunnel running into the East Hill provoking inevitable tales of smuggling, while no. 127 is more precisely dated as being built in 1540. The house called Shovells, at no. 125, has a firemark on the wall and is part of a 15th century Wealden hall house, as are nos. 51 and 58-60.

There are peculiarities, too. The so-called 'Piece of Cheese' house, appropriately painted yellow, is an unfailing tourists' delight near the foot of the street. Its unusual shape emphasises the perennial Old Town problem of fitting buildings into meagre space.

Stranger still, however, its Pulpitt Gate, named after the postern gate that once stood in the town wall at this spot. This is a 1950's concoction, with fake timber-framing and a huge stone window taken from the ruin of Normanhurst, the French-style chateau which the railway engineer Thomas Brassey built for himself at Catsfield, near Battle. Inside, there are stained glass windows, a Jacobean staircase and (in the dining room of all places) a disused well.

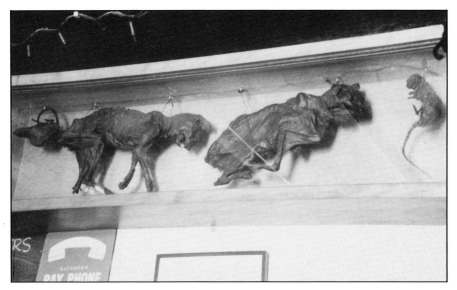

These blackened, mummified cats were discovered in a chimney at the Stag Inn during restoration work.

All Saints Street is rich in old buildings, some disguising their age behind later facades.

Shovells, maintained by the Sussex Archaeological Society, has an old firemark above its dormer window.

Nos. 58-60 All Saints Street. The pavement here is raised well above the road.

Pleasant Row, at the foot of Saints Street. The old town wall survives as the foundations of the back walls of these buildings.

This giant winkle at the foot of All Saints Street advertises the charitable Winkle Club, formed in 1899 to help underprivileged families in the town.

HASTINGS

The Fishing Quarter

Tall, black wooden sheds known as the net shops draw the eye towards the Stade (from the Old English for shore or landing place), which for centuries past has been the centre of the fishermen's beach. The Stade once lay closer to the foot of High Street than it does today, but the harbour arm and several large groynes have caused a large build-up of shingle and pushed the beach further south. While other fishing fleets have practically disappeared from the East Sussex coast, Hastings retains a vigorous industry — and a public auction held most mornings for early risers.

East from the Stade a short road runs under the East Hill to Rock-a-Nore (or 'the Mayne Rocke against the north', as a report of 1581 described it). Here there are no fewer than three maritime attractions within a few hundred yards, one of them telling the story of Hastings fishermen in their former chapel of ease. The rock itself is pock-marked with caves which have been inhabited at various times in the past. Water continually seeps from it and is basined in the East Well, a structure which dates from 1846 though there was a water supply here long before that.

Within living memory the fishermen had a distinctive vocabulary of their own. There are few traces of it now, but the fishing community retains a proud spirit of independence.

ROCK-A-NORE ATTRACTIONS

Shipwreck Heritage Centre (Easter to October, daily) 0424 437452

Fishermen's Museum (late May to September, limited hours)

Sealife Centre (all year, daily) 0424 718776

The distinctive shape of the net shops may date from Tudor times.

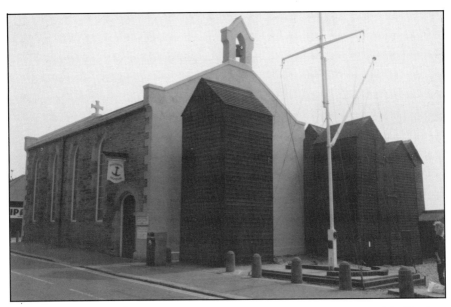

The Fishermen's Museum, a chapel of ease from 1854 until 1939, has the last of the Hastings luggers on view. A wall had to be dismantled in order to get the boat in.

There are some 500 known shipwrecks in the Dover Straits, most of them from after 1850, and this grim aspect of local history is explored at the Shipwreck Heritage Centre. Note the cross and belfry of the Fishermen's Museum in the background.

A box of muskets in the Shipwreck Heritage Centre. It was recovered from the 'tombstone wreck', so called because its cargo included a tombstone being shipped abroad to an Englishman's last resting place.

'Waste not, want not' reads the plaque on the East Well. In former times this cistern was the only reliable pure water supply in the Old Town.

The caves in the honeycombed sandstone rocks of the East Hill provided dry homes for poor families and their animals during the 19th century. The local council drove out 'hippies' with similar intentions during the 1960s.

East Hill cliffs and fishing quarter.

THE *AMSTERDAM*

Perhaps the most celebrated of all the shipwrecks off the Sussex coast is that of the Dutch East Indiaman *Amsterdam,* beached between Hastings and Bexhill on January 26, 1749. She had set sail on her maiden voyage a little more than two weeks before, bound for Java with a cargo of silver, wine and cloth. The crew were for the most part poor and undernourished men, and when a fever began to spread in the insanitary conditions below deck they were soon dying at the rate of five a day. As if that were not enough, the *Amsterdam* had no sooner entered the English Channel than she was savaged by a violent gale: driven into Pevensey Bay, she struck the seabed and lost her rudder. The captain was all for sailing on, but the crew seems to have mutinied, breaking into the liquor supplies and running the ship ashore. The wreck can be seen at very low tides off Bulverhythe, and some of the artefacts recovered by marine archaeologists are on display at the Shipwreck Heritage Centre.

For those in peril: the Hastings lifeboat (the 38ft Mersey class Sealink Endeavour) is housed to the west of the fishing quarter. The lifeboat house also serves as a museum.

Piledriving during March 1984 to provide a protective underwater dam around the Amsterdam, embedded in Hastings sand.

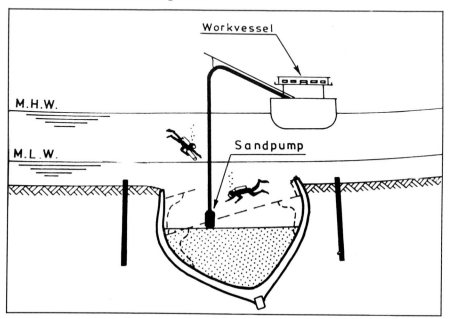

Sketch showing excavation by volunteer divers, Summer 1984.

HASTINGS

Hastings Country Park

To travel from the huddled antiquity of the Old Town to the bracing open landscape of Hastings Country Park requires not only an imaginative leap but a ride in the vertiginous East Hill lift (the steepest in Britain) or the climbing of no fewer than 272 steps. There is, indeed, history here, too — this has been officially declared an 'area of archaeological importance', with parts of it scheduled as an ancient monument — but the obvious glories of the five mile swathe from the East Hill to Cliff End near Pett are natural ones: clattering streams; woods and heathland; acres of blazing gorse across the aptly-named Firehills; deep glens which cut through crumbling sandstone to issue at the sea's edge.

From Fairlight church the early 19th century historian Mark Antony Lower calculated that a visitor could see fifteen towns, 67 churches, five castles, 60 martello towers and 40 windmills. The tally is rather different today, but the church stands higher above sea level than any in Sussex (at 599ft) and still offers the best panoramic views of the 1066 Country.

There are nature trails across the Firehills and through Ecclesbourne, Fairlight and Warren Glens: leaflets are available from the Country Park interpretive centre off Fairlight Road.

The East Hill lift, completed in 1903 and originally water-powered, climbs a gradient of 1:1.28. It was balanced by 600-gallon water tanks until its electrification in 1974.

Hastings Country Park, looking east towards Ecclesbourne Glen. The 600-acre site is important for both naturalists and historians.

HASTINGS

The Tackleway Area

At the very east of the Old Town, hard against the East Cliff and running down from All Saints Church to Rock-a-Nore via Tamarisk Steps, is a road whose name seems to smack of the fishing industry. In fact, Tackleway is written as 'le tegill wey' in a deed of 1499 and seems to refer to medieval tile kilns.

The road was made up in 1852, having been 'a most dangerous thoroughfare', and the large houses built at the top of it before that date had their entrances in All Saints Street. East Hill House, built for James Wenham, was often let out to visitors, including (as a plaque proclaims) George III's son Augustus Frederic, Duke of Sussex. Hastings House, since demolished, numbered among its guests the Duke of Wellington (when the area was the first line of defence against possible invasion by Napoleon Bonaparte) and the poet Lord Byron.

It was, no doubt, inevitable that the grounds of both these houses should later be built over in response to the demands of a growing population. Indeed, the whole area between Tackleway and All Saints Street is a typical Old Town townscape of tightly-packed houses on terraces carved out of the steep hillside; see, in particular, the attractive cottages along Wood's Passage and Strong's Passage, which were built in the back gardens of houses in All Saints Street.

Just above Tamarisk Steps (with a convenient seat for the leg-weary) is the Lookout. It's an excellent spot for looking down on the Stade and Rock-a-Nore, and was traditionally the favourite gathering place for fishermen's wives and children anxious to see their menfolk returning safety from sea.

A fragment of the original medieval town wall, behind the Royal Standard Inn.

How to use every square inch: Trafalgar Cottages off Tackleway.

A general view of Tackleway, formerly 'the tile way'.

Mulberries à la Shakespeare! A gate to your left as you climb Tamarisk Steps leads to a garden which used to belong to East Cliff House in All Saints Street. During the 1770s the Shakespearian scholar Edward Capel lived here, and the actor David Garrick brought him what he claimed to be a cutting from the bard's own mulberry tree at Stratford-on-Avon. This ancient tree is still flourishing.

THE ARMS OF HASTINGS

Per pale gules and azure; a lion passant guardant Or between in chief and in base a lion passant guardant of the third conjoined to an ancient ship's hull Argent.

The Arms of the Cinque Ports have three lions dimidated with three ship's hulls. Dimidation means joining half of one shield — in this case the three lions of England — to half of another: three ships. Only Hastings retains the middle lion complete. The reason for this difference, which makes the arms of Hastings unique, is lost in the mists of time. (*See back cover*)

HASTINGS

The Tourist Trade

Despite its obvious attractions for visitors, Hastings has never had a settled philosophy regarding the tourism on which it obviously depends. In the early days that was unimportant; the 'quality' discovered the town during the Napoleonic period, and it grew with little need for encouragement until, in the 1880s, it was second in size only to Brighton among Sussex resorts. Later, however, its distance from the capital compared with both Brighton and the Kent coast meant that strenuous efforts were required to give the town what would today be termed 'a corporate image'. Should it offer the upmarket demeanour of an Eastbourne or the more boisterous pleasures of a Margate or a Southend? In the event no decision was made at all, to the despair of many critics over the past hundred years.

The consequences of this long-term neglect are all about us. For one thing, there is an obvious clash between opposing tourist cultures: quite apart from its natural advantages of cliffs and sea, Hastings is blessed with a legacy of fine historic buildings, yet the sprawling amusement arcades along the eastern shore seems to advertise a different kind of resort altogether. For another, a decline in tourist numbers has led to an inevitable dwindling of investment in the town: too long a journey from London for massive incursions of day-trippers, Hastings lacks the hotels which would encourage other kinds of visitors to stay. Its fate, in short, has been to become shabby without being in the least genteel.

Can the decline be reversed? The completion of the channel tunnel, offering the possibility of a surge in visitors from Europe, has at long last concentrated civic minds. Investors are being encouraged to anticipate a recovery. A promotions company is working on a suitable strategy. Perhaps it is not too late to hope that an area 'popular with visitors since 1066' may, against all the odds, become more popular than ever in the twenty-first century.

The area of seafront close to the harbour arm at Hastings has become a large, and popular, amusements area. But is it in conflict with the 'heritage' image the town wishes to promote?

The boating lake.

HASTINGS

Georgian Hastings

It was a stroke of luck that several of our Sussex seaside resorts began to be developed late in the 18th century, for it has bequeathed them touches of that elegance which is synonymous with Georgian architecture. Hastings may not possess the sheer quantity which Brighton can boast, but Wellington Square (from 1815) and Pelham Crescent (1824, with the church of St. Mary-in-the-Castle as its centrepiece) would be welcomed wherever they were to be found.

Although the supposed health-giving quality of sea-water was the chief enticement to visitors, it soon became essential to provide amusements for those large parts of the day and evening when they were not bathing in the briny or, as recommended by some doctors, drinking it. The first assembly rooms were opened at the Swan Inn, near St. Clement's Church, in 1771, and within a few years there were two libraries offering not only books and newspapers, but music and billiards, too. Warm baths were built after 1800, the town's first theatre (now the Hare & Hounds pub) opened in great Bourne Street in 1825, and pleasure-boating, horse-racing and a regatta became regular summer entertainments. The caves on the West Hill were established as a tourist attraction in July 1827.

The years around the turn of the century were, of course, a time of war and threatened invasion. Between 1794 and 1814 cavalry, dragoons and militiamen were continuously camped in and around the town, providing a boost to the local economy and a colourful entertainment all their own, but also bringing the obvious problems of overcrowding, rowdiness and reckless sexual adventure. Three martello towers were built as coastal defences in the Hastings area, and notable soldiers to be billeted in the town included Sir John Moore (who later fell at Corunna) and Sir Arthur Wellesley, later the Duke of Wellington.

Despite all this martial activity, the 'season' continued unabated. Some visitors came by sea, but most had to endure travelling the notoriously uncomfortable Sussex roads. In the late 18th century, with Hastings becoming increasingly recognised as a fashionable resort, there were several coaches a week to and from the capital, completing the journey in one long day. By the 1830s the creation of turnpike trusts had led to some improvement in the state of the roads, and keen competition between various carriers had reduced travelling times and brought fares down. It is not at all difficult to understand, however, how welcome the railway was to be when it eventually arrived at St. Leonards in 1841.

Wellington Square, begun in 1815, is one of the town's finest Georgian creations.

Named for the church inside the castle which it replaced, St. Mary's is a remarkable creation built on the sandstone rock. Designed by Joseph Kay, it has a galleried horse-shoe shaped auditorium which is lit from above. A natural spring which runs through it once fed a font for baptisms by total immersion. The church is open on Sunday afternoons during restoration.

Pelham Crescent, built for the Earl of Chichester, presses hard against the West Hill, part of which was demolished to make room for it. The church of St. Mary-in-the-Castle is its centrepiece.

The weather-worn lion and unicorn at either end of Robertson Terrace were originally commissioned for Buckingham Palace — a reminder that this part of the town is Crown Estate.

HASTINGS

The New Town

Coastal towns can grow in only three directions at most, and what we now know as the Old Town of Hastings was further restricted by the barriers of the East and West Hills. A walk in that area shows how imaginatively every available space was used for cramming in as many houses as possible, but an overspilling of the population to the west was inevitable as the town's popularity grew during the 19th century. George Street was densely colonised, and the cliff was cut away under the castle to allow the building of Pelham Crescent, but the heart of the new town was to be in the Priory Valley area between the West Hill and White Rock. The present town hall was built here in 1881, replacing what is now the local history museum in High Street. The former county cricket ground at Priory Meadow occupies the supposed site of the former port of Hastings, long since silted up and covered over.

The development of the area was decidedly piecemeal. During the early years of the town's expansion the area was settled by squatters, who resisted attempts by the authorities to remove their unsightly and unhygienic shanty town, hoisting the Stars and Stripes flag in defiance: the land became known as the America Ground. In 1834, following a legal ruling that this was Crown Estate, the inhabitants

The shopping centre of Hastings, partly pedestrianised in the early 1990s. The area at the centre of the picture is still known as the Memorial, although the statue of Prince Albert which once stood here (see facing page) was taken down more than twenty years ago.

The town hall, in Queen's Road, houses the Hastings Embroidery, a modern Bayeux Tapestry created to mark the 900th anniversary of the Norman Conquest. More than 240ft long, and in 27 panels, it depicts eighty of the great events and characters of British history since the Battle of Hastings. A plaque in Queen's Arcade, nearby, records that John Logie Baird transmitted the first television pictures from a workshop here in 1924.

were served with notices to quit. Their response was to shift their settlement further west, taking their ramshackle homes with them.

Some fifteen years after this reluctant evacuation the wealthy London merchant Patrick Robertson took a 99-year lease on the America Ground and set about developing it as a high-class resort. The modern centre of Hastings has been fleshed out on the skeleton of Robertson's scheme. Not all of his plans came to fruition (and German bombs were to destroy the Albany Hotel and the surrounding area during the second world war), but Robertson Street and Terrace, Holy Trinity Church and the Queen's Hotel are among the many survivors from that period.

Prince Albert Memorial. A Victorian legacy which has since been removed was the memorial to Prince Albert, a 65ft high landmark erected in 1862. It stood in Harold Place until 1973, when it was damaged by fire and then dismantled to make way for road improvements.

HASTINGS

The White Rock

Until 1835 a large, bleached sandstone headland sufficiently substantial to house a coastguards look-out thrust towards the sea west of the so-called America Ground. At high tide it was impossible to pass in front of it, and in that year the White Rock was blown up with gunpowder in order to make room for the town's relentless expansion west. A new road and seafront promenade were created, and new buildings quickly sprang up alongside them.

The outcome was not entirely beneficial. The White Rock had served as a protective bastion against the fury of the sea, and the following autumn saw serious flooding in the Priory Valley. The Priory stream ran through what is now Alexandra Park (as it still does) and then meandered to the sea through marshland: a consequence of the White Rock's demolition was that decisions were now taken to strengthen the Priory bridge and to drain the marshes by piping the stream through a culvert to the sea.

The White Rock was the last frontier, for Hastings was now on course to meet its new neighbour, St. Leonards. Today this area is an entertainment centre, with a theatre (standing a little to the west of the demolished headland from which it gets its name) and a pier designed by that creator of many similar Victorian masterpieces, Eugenius Birch.

Hastings Pier, designed by Eugenius Birch, was built in 1872 and stretches 910ft out to sea.

The White Rock Theatre.

Bottle Alley, a covered promenade, stretches half a mile from the pier to Warrior Square. It was built in 1933 and is decorated with many thousands of pieces of broken glass.

ST. LEONARDS

Although St. Leonards, like Hastings, has sprawled formlessly during the past hundred years, it retains at its heart the essence of the elegant seaside town planned by James Burton in the 1820s. Burton, a London builder who had houses, villas and terraces in fashionable parts of London to his name, began developing St. Leonards in 1828. His architect son Decimus continued the work after his death.

The showpieces of the new town were the St. Leonards Hotel (later re-named the Royal Victoria after the Queen, who had visited the town as a girl) and the assembly rooms close by (now the Masonic Hall). Burton also created the beautiful gardens, then open only to subscribers, which run down towards the sea from Maze Hill: the maze for which it is named is, alas, long gone.

The Mercatoria area, at the eastern side of the town, was built as the shopping district for the working classes, whose thirst ensured that the Horse and Groom pub was doing a good trade even before its windows had been glazed. The pretty row of cottages along nearby Norman Road was part of the laundry area, known as Lavatoria.

Many of the Burtons' original buildings remain, including Allegria Court, James Burton's own home in the years before his death. The distinctive family mausoleum, pyramidal in shape, is to be found in a small graveyard off West Hill Road, above St. Leonards church.

Warrior Square. A hoard of Roman coins was discovered while the foundations of houses on the west side were being dug in 1855.

Crown House (no. 57 Marina) was the first house to be built at St. Leonards — as James Burton's own home. It was made in his London workshop and transported in sections by sea.

James Burton's pyramidal mausoleum squats on the clifftop above the town he created. The modern church of St. Leonards, seen behind it, replaced the old parish church which was reduced to rubble by a V-1 flying bomb on the night of July 29, 1944.

Marine Court rises like a beached liner behind eastern St. Leonards, dwarfing Burton's classical colonnade. Thirteen storeys high, and obviously 1930s in design, it has a 'promenade deck' on the top floor.

The Royal Victoria Hotel was designed as the centrepiece of Burton's design for St. Leonards.

North Lodge was built as the northern entrance to James Burton's new town. The writer Sir Henry Rider Haggard, author of King Solomon's Mines, *lived here after the first world war.*

The gothic Clock House overlooks the St. Leonards Gardens, which were originally open only to subscribers. A special feature of these attractive gardens is the provision of plant name-plates in braille for blind visitors.

BEXHILL

The growth of modern Bexhill began late in the Victorian period, when the De La Warr family developed it as a seaside resort, but a stroll through the Old Town shows that the place has a much longer history than that: indeed, St. Peter's stands on land specifically granted by King Offa for the building of a church as long ago as 772AD. There's an unusual pair of semi-detached Wealden hall houses by the lych gate, while the ruins close to the church are those of the manor house which Bishop Adam de Molayns was given permission to embattle in 1450.

It wasn't until the threat of Napoleonic invasion brought large numbers of troops to the town that Bexhill first began to expand. Barrack Hall, at one end of the short High Street, served as the officers' mess when the King's German Legion was quartered here, and several Georgian buildings in the Old Town date from this turbulent period. Hundreds of soldiers and their families lie in unmarked graves in the old cemetery in Barrack Road.

Starting in the 1880s, the seventh Earl De La Warr built the sea wall, laid out parades and introduced efficient gas and water supplies. The architect Sir Ernest George built large houses with Dutch gables, many of which still survive. The eighth Earl later took up where his father had left off, until Bexhill was in the forefront of English resorts, with a zesty reputation which seems a little surprising today: in 1901 it was the first in England to allow mixed bathing, while a year later it became the first town in the country to organise motor racing trials.

The De La Warr Pavilion, the town's main entertainments centre, was designed by the Germans Mendelsohn and Chermayeff in the 1930s and appears in most books of modern architecture.

The Bexhill Stone, discovered under the nave floor during a 19th century restoration, is thought to be the lid of a reliquary — a container for the relics of a saint. It may have been placed in the original church more than 1200 years ago.

The Old Town of Bexhill, with a view part way up Church Street. St. Peter's lychgate can be seen directly in front of the church, with an unusual pair of semi-detached Wealden hall houses to its right. The timber-clad building in the foreground is a former grainstore, its clock a Queen Victoria jubilee commemoration.

Bexhill Manor ruins. The terracing of the gardens probably dates from around 1450, when Bishop Adam de Molayns was given permission to embattle his house as a measure against raids by the French. In the old stables is a museum of costume and social history, with tableaux from the 18th century to the present.

The De La Warr Pavilion on Bexhill sea front is acclaimed by architects as one of the finest buildings of its era.

PEVENSEY AND WESTHAM

It's difficult to imagine the sea slapping against the walls of Pevensey Castle, but so it did some 1700 years ago when the Romans built a stronghold here to keep Saxon pirates at bay. The Roman walls, considerably patched up, are the ones you see as you approach the castle. Formidable as they may have been, they were unable to withstand Saxon assaults once the Roman legions had withdrawn from Britain, and the *Anglo Saxon Chronicle* for 491 records that every last inhabitant was killed in a decisive battle here.

The Conqueror lands at Pevensey: from the Bayeux Tapestry — 11th century.
(Reproduced with the special authorisation of the town of Bayeux)

Saxon Pevensey was an important port town, having its own mint, and it was an obvious target for the Normans after they had landed nearby in 1066. The sea had evidently not yet retreated to leave the place high and dry, for soon after his victory over Harold, the Conqueror built a new castle inside the walls of the Roman one. The town later became a member of the Cinque Ports federation.

Pevensey's high street, now mercifully bypassed, is packed with interesting buildings. The 16th century Court House, which later served as the smallest town hall in England, is now a museum of local history.

Neighbouring Westham may not have as long a history, but it does lay claim to possessing the first church to be built in England after the Conquest. St. Mary's has original Norman work in its south wall and the Lady Chapel, and a massive tower of flint and stone which was added during the 14th century.

Elizabethan demi-culverin at Pevensey Castle.

The Normans built their castle in the south-east corner of the Roman fort at Pevensey. The gatehouse at the left of the picture contains some original work, but the curtain wall and drum tower to the right were built in the mid-13th century.

Westham church: perhaps the first to be built by the Normans after 1066.

The church of St. Nicholas, Pevensey.

The Court House, which has a local history museum on its first floor, has been called 'the smallest town hall in England'. It no longer serves that function, of course, but it certainly was a town hall in the days of Pevensey's greatness. There was a council chamber on the upper floor and a prison below — and the cells can still be visited.

North and East towers, Pevensey Castle.

BATTLE & THE NORMAN CONQUEST

The most famous of English battles takes its name from the fact that Hastings was then the nearest settlement of any size, but the gruelling, day-long conflict between the forces of King Harold and the invading Normans actually took place at Senlac Hill, some six miles to the north-west. The battlefield can be walked today, on the slopes beneath the ruins of the great Benedictine abbey which William ordered to be built in thanksgiving for his victory.

Strategic noticeboards help to bring the battle to life, showing where Harold and his housecarls, occupying a dominating ridge, were assailed by a terrifying hail of arrows from William's archers. A stone marks the high altar of the abbey church, built (rather gloatingly, one feels) at the spot where Harold fell.

Although the abbey was to be dismantled when Henry VIII closed the monasteries, the gatehouse of about 1340 remains, as does the shell of the monks' dormitory with a series of vaulted rooms beneath. Sir Anthony Browne, who acquired the abbey at the Dissolution, retained the abbot's house for his own use and this, with later additions, is now a girls' school.

Battle now seems the least industrial of small towns, but from 1676 until 1874 the area had some of the largest gunpowder mills in England. The remnants of workshops, a powder packing house and a blacksmith's forge can be seen to the south of the town beside the large pond which provided the enterprise with its water-power. Perhaps because of this explosive past, the town has long been known for its bonfire celebrations, enlivened by the deafening fireworks known as Battle Rousers.

ATTRACTIONS IN BATTLE

Battle Abbey: open all year 04246 3792

Buckley's Yesterday's World (shops museum), near the Abbey: open all year 04246 4269

Battle Historical Museum, near the Abbey: open Easter-early October 04246 2044

Town model, The Almonry, top of High Street: open all year 04246 2727

Battle High Street, from the Abbey. The vintage van belongs to one of the local attractions, Buckley's Yesterday's World. A plaque in the small car park on the left marks the spot where bull-baiting took place in earlier times.

The Abbey gatehouse, which dates from the early 14th century. The photograph has been taken inside the grounds.

The most atmospheric part of the abbey remains is the 13th century undercroft of the monks' dormitory. The style is Early English.

Stone slab marking the location of the high altar of Battle Abbey — the very spot where King Harold fell.

Buckley's Yesterday's World.

WINCHELSEA

Here, thanks largely to the fickleness of the elements, we have a rare example of 13th century town planning practically in aspic. Even before the old town of Winchelsea was finally washed away by storms in 1287, Edward I had ordered the building of a new settlement on higher ground. His planners created wharves below the northern cliff, alongside the (then much wider) River Brede, and they laid out the streets on a grid pattern unique in England.

It was to be a substantial town, as may be judged by the three sturdy stone gateways which survive, not to speak of the large cellars which still exist below what were once warehouses for prosperous merchants. Winchelsea, in medieval times, was a busy trading port and a leading member of the Confederation of Cinque Ports, and there seemed no reason to doubt that the new town would be just as successful as the one it replaced. That dream was to be shattered, however, by two different agencies: French marauders, who carried out a succession of murderous raids all along this part of the Sussex coast and, once again, the sea, which this time withdrew and left the town stranded. Only a part of King Edward's grid was ever completed.

Winchelsea now sank into centuries of poverty, during which the Methodist preacher John Wesley notably described it 'that poor skeleton': he was here in 1790 to give what was to be his last open air sermon, and a plaque by an ash tree outside the churchyard marks the spot. By this time the merchants were long gone, the remaining buildings were in a state of disrepair and grass was growing in the streets.

That long neglect, paradoxically, accounts for the quality which visitors most appreciate in today's Winchelsea: its sense of being out of time. You feel it in the unfinished church with its ancient tombs. You feel it when you look east from the Lookout across the bleak marshes. The surviving houses have been restored now, but the small criss-crossing of roads remains such as it was all those centuries ago. Here you leave the restless modern world behind.

The Strand Gate, Winchelsea, built early in the 14th century.

The stone-built Court Hall, dating from the 14th century, is almost as old as Winchelsea itself. A museum on the top floor tells the story of a town which is the smallest in England to have its own mayor and corporation.

Winchelsea's town well, built in 1831, was in use within living memory. One of its two notice boards gives its former opening times (6a.m. to 7p.m. but closed on the Sabbath), while the other gives a warning: 'All persons are strictly cautioned against throwing anything whatsoever down the town well as the Police have order to report immediately any act of nuisance so that the offenders may be prosecuted.'

The intended size of Winchelsea church may be gauged by the fact that what we see is nothing more than the chancel and side chapels. Whether much more was ever completed is open to doubt: if it was, then almost certainly the French destroyed it. Despite its incompleteness, however, the church has an undeniable grandeur — and an atmosphere that seems to impress itself on every visitor. It was outside the church wall that John Wesley preached his last open-air sermon, and a plaque records the fact.

Looking towards Rye, with lock gates to the Royal Military Canal in the foreground.

*The Ypres Tower (*see next page*) and River Rother, Rye.*

RYE

There is no Sussex town quite like Rye, which stands high above the surrounding marshes on its sandstone hill, its surviving medieval defences suggesting how impregnable it must have seemed when the sea lapped its feet rather than languishing, as it does now, a few miles away. Inside the remnants of the ancient walls, a host of timber-framed and Georgian houses clamber up the hillside either side of narrow, often cobbled, streets.

The impressively large warehouses at Strand Quay are a relic of the town's past as a powerful shipbuilding and seafaring town, the Ypres Tower of 1250 a reminder of the ever-present danger of attacks from France. Rye's story mirrors Winchelsea's in that it was practically destroyed by the French during the 14th century and, after having its eastern part washed away, was later killed as a port by falling sea-levels. Despite these vicissitudes, a small fishing fleet still survives.

Among the many fine buildings to look out for are the 15th century Fletcher's House (where the Elizabethan dramatist is said to have been born) close to the church; the Old Grammar School in the High Street (1636, with Dutch gables and giant pilasters); and Lamb House at the top of Mermaid Street (built in 1723 by James Lamb, whose family was to provide the town's mayor on no fewer than seventy-eight occasions). Lamb House was the home of two very different writers: the American novelist Henry James and the author of the Mapp and Lucia books, E.F. Benson.

ATTRACTIONS IN RYE

Ypres Tower Museum (near the church) open Easter to mid-October 0797 223254

Rye Heritage Centre & Town Model, Strand Quay, open April to October and winter weekends 0797 226696

Lamb House (National Trust) open April to October, Wednesday and Saturday afternoons 0797 223763

Rye Art Gallery, open all year Tuesday to Saturday 0797 222433

The Land Gate at Rye. The clock is a memorial to Prince Albert, installed in 1863.

The 13th-century Ypres Tower, with the Gun Garden in the foreground.

St. Mary's Church, seen from Lion Street. The end arcade of the town hall can be seen in front of the church.

The church clock, dating from 1561, has a quotation from the Apocrypha above it: 'For our time is a very shadow that passeth away.' The quarterboys strike the quarters as their name suggests, but not the full hours.

This remarkable cistern, or water house, sits in the churchyard and was built in 1735 to store water pumped up Conduit Hill from Cinque Ports Street. Local households were then supplied through a network of pipes running downhill. The structure is oval, yet made entirely of brick: a real feat of bricklaying artistry.

The Mermaid Inn was a haunt of the notorious Hawkhurst Gang of smugglers.

Friars of the Sack in Church Square. All the early timber buildings of Rye were destroyed in assaults by the French during the 14th and 15th centuries, and the partial survival of this house is a result of its being built of solid stone. The friary was founded around 1263 and dissolved some forty years later. The remains of the Austin Friars can be seen in Conduit Hill.

The 15th century Fletcher's House is the supposed birthplace of the Elizabethan dramatist, better known as part of the tandem 'Beaumont and Fletcher'. The narrow frontage was originally the side of the house. The old front door has been filled in, but you can still see (if you squeeze between the two buildings in the picture) the moulded fascia board over the jetty and the spandrels with their pleasing foliage design.

THE VILLAGES OF 1066 COUNTRY

The villages and hamlets of the 1066 country are to be enjoyed at leisure, with ancient churches and clusters of tile-hung and weather-boarded houses hidden away down winding narrow lanes: the beautiful composition of church, manor house and farm buildings at *Penhurst,* west of Battle, is a prime example of such hidden treasures.

There is also a wide range of attractions which are more obviously in the public eye, among them castles of different periods in English history. The one at *Bodiam,* a picture-book shell within a moat, was begun in 1385 as a defence against French pirates who could then sail all the way inland up to the broad River Brede. *Herstmonceux* Castle, some way to the west of Hastings, was built of brick about half a century later, while the elaborate gun-platform at *Camber* (now stranded inland, and in the process of being restored by English Heritage), was the only Sussex castle to be built by Henry VIII.

Of all the vineyards which have sprung up in Sussex during the past few years, the biggest is David Carr Taylor's at *Westfield,* which offers tours and wine-tastings, but there's also an organic vineyard at *Sedlescombe* — a village which has an attractive green complete with well-house and pump, and counts the Pestalozzi Children's Village as a near neighbour.

There are houses to visit, too. Great Dixter at *Northiam* (where a sign on the village green marks the oak tree under which the first Queen Elizabeth enjoyed a picnic) is actually two timber-framed medieval houses in one with beautiful grounds managed by the gardening writer Christopher Lloyd. Bateman's, at *Burwash,* is a former ironmaster's house which became the home of Rudyard Kipling.

Museums in the area include Ripley's Museum of Rural Life at *Robertsbridge,* a village which is also home to the cricket bat manufacturers Gray-Nicholls.

Herstmonceux Castle.

Bodiam Castle in its moat. Powerful cannon were to make it obsolete almost as soon as it was completed at the end of the 14th century.

Two medieval hall houses in one. In 1910 the owner of Great Dixter bought a similar house in Kent and had it transported here, attaching it to his original property: both can be seen in the picture. Sir Edwin Lutyens advised on the architecture and laid out the garden.

A relic of World War II: tank obstructions around the perimeter of a field near Sedlescombe.

Bateman's at Burwash was built for a Wealden iron master. It was later the home of the writer Rudyard Kipling, who set many of his stories and poems in Sussex. It's owned by the National Trust.

INDEX